CRÊPES, SOUFFLÉS & OMELETS

Edited by
Rhona Newman

Contents

NOTES

Standard spoon measurements are used in all recipes
1 tablespoon = one 15 ml spoon
1 teaspoon = one 5 ml spoon
All spoon measures are level.

Fresh herbs are used unless otherwise stated. If unobtainable, substitute a bouquet garni of the equivalent dried herbs, or use dried herbs instead but halve the quantities stated.

Use freshly ground black pepper where pepper is specified.

Ovens and grills (broilers) should be preheated to the specified temperature or heat setting.

For all recipes, quantities are given in metric, imperial and American measures. Follow one set of measures only, because they are not interchangeable.

This edition first published 1981 by
Octopus Books Limited
59 Grosvenor Street, London W1

© 1981 Octopus Books Limited

ISBN 0 7064 1477 2

Produced by Mandarin Publishers Ltd
22a Westlands Rd
Quarry Bay, Hong Kong
Printed in Hong Kong

Frontispiece: AUBERGINE (EGGPLANT) SOUFFLÉS *(page 51)*
(Photograph: Carmel Produce Information Service)

INTRODUCTION

Crêpes, soufflés and omelets all use the versatile egg to produce an endless variety of tasty, nutritious dishes.

OMELETS

There are three basic types of omelet, to which different flavourings and fillings can be added. The French or plain omelet is the most familiar kind and is generally savoury. It is usually served folded, either plain or enclosing a filling. The soufflé omelet, sometimes known as the fluffy omelet, has a lighter texture because the egg whites are separated, whisked and folded into the mixture before cooking. Soufflé omelets can be filled with sweet or savoury fillings. Spanish omelets are more substantial because they contain plenty of extra ingredients. They are always served flat, cut into wedges.

Omelet pans: Ideally a pan should be kept solely for omelets so it need not be washed after use. If the pan is washed, it may cause sticking. An omelet pan with a non-stick surface is the easiest to use, but ordinary cast iron and aluminium pans also give good results. The omelet pan should be about 5 cm/2 inches deep with a thick base and curved sides to make the omelet easier to turn out.

If you buy an omelet pan without a non-stick surface, 'prove' it before use: Wash and dry thoroughly, then cover the base with olive or cooking oil to a depth of 0.5 cm/¼ inch. Heat the pan slowly to smoking point, then remove from the heat and leave to stand for 12 hours. Pour off the oil and wipe with absorbent kitchen paper.

Thereafter you need not wash the pan again. After use, simply wipe it round with a damp cloth or absorbent kitchen paper, dipped in salt. This will season the pan and prevent it from sticking.

For an individual 2 egg omelet, a 15-18 cm/6-7 inch pan is the most convenient size to use. For a 3-4 egg omelet sufficient to serve two people, an 18-20 cm/7-8 inch omelet pan is better. Spanish omelets normally require a larger frying pan (skillet).

Hints for Successful Omelet-Making

1. Use absolutely fresh eggs at room temperature.
2. Have ingredients prepared and equipment ready beforehand.
3. Always season savoury omelets before cooking, not afterwards.
4. Cook plain and soufflé omelets over moderate heat; cook Spanish omelets over low heat.
5. Melt the butter in the omelet pan and wait until it is foaming, but not discoloured, before adding the egg mixture.
6. For plain omelets, pour in the egg mixture all at once. Leave for 15 to 20 seconds, stir using the back of a fork, then leave again for 5 seconds. Draw in the edges of the omelet to allow any remaining raw egg mixture to run around the edges and cook.
7. Never overcook, and always serve immediately after cooking.

CRÊPES

Crêpes, or pancakes, are traditionally eaten on Shrove Tuesday – the day before Lent. In days past, when it was customary to fast during Lent, surplus eggs, flour and milk were saved until Shrove Tuesday and made into crêpes. However, filled with sweet or savoury fillings, they are far too good to be eaten on just one day of the year.

The basic batter is quick and easy to make, whether you use an electric blender, food processor, or simply a wooden spoon to combine the ingredients. The resulting batter should have the consistency of smooth cream.

For cooking crêpes, use a non-stick frying pan (skillet), or one which has been proved (see omelet pans). You will also need a little vegetable oil, a spatula and a jug for pouring the batter. If the crêpes are to be eaten straight away, have the filling ready.

Basic Crêpe Batter

These quantities are sufficient to make 300 ml/½ pint (1¼ cups). For an enriched batter, add an extra egg. Unless otherwise stated, this is the amount of batter required to make the crêpes in each recipe.

METRIC/IMPERIAL	AMERICAN
100 g/4 oz plain flour	*1 cup all-purpose flour*
½ teaspoon salt	*½ teaspoon salt*
1 egg	*1 egg*
300 ml/½ pint milk	*1¼ cups milk*

Sift the flour and salt into a bowl. Make a well in the centre and add the egg and one third of the milk. Stir, drawing the flour in from the sides, then beat well until smooth. Gradually blend in the remaining milk and transfer the mixture to a jug.

Crêpe Quantities from 300 ml/½ pint (1¼ cups) batter

Diameter of pan	Number of crêpes
13 cm/5 inches	12
15 cm/6 inches	10
18 cm/7 inches	8
20 cm/8 inches	6
23 cm/9 inches	4

To cook crêpes: Heat the frying pan (skillet) over moderate heat, then wipe with an oiled piece of cloth or absorbent kitchen paper. Pour in sufficient batter to just cover the base, tilting the pan to spread evenly. Cook gently, without moving, until the underside of the crêpe is golden. Toss or turn, using a spatula or palette knife and cook the other side for about 15 seconds until golden. Slide onto a warmed plate and keep hot. Repeat with the remaining batter.

PREPARING AND WRAPPING CRÊPES FOR THE FREEZER
(Photograph: Bacofoil Limited)

Stacking crêpes: To keep crêpes warm while cooking more of them, stack flat, interleaved with sheets of greaseproof (wax) paper on a warmed plate. Cover with foil and place in a very cool oven.

Storing crêpes: Unfilled crêpes can be stored in the refrigerator for up to 5 days. Layer them between sheets of greaseproof (wax) paper, then wrap in foil.

Crêpes may also be stored in the freezer. Stack and wrap in convenient quantities as for refrigerator storage, then place in a polythene bag, seal, label and freeze for up to 4 months.

Stuffed crêpes can also be frozen for about 2 months, depending on the filling. They should be packed in rigid containers.

Reheating crêpes: Crêpes are best thawed at room temperature. Stacked crêpes will take 2-3 hours; separated ones will take about 15 minutes.

To reheat, place stacks of no more than 6 crêpes, wrapped in foil, in a preheated cool oven (150°C/300°F, Gas Mark 2) for about 30 minutes. Alternatively, reheat individual pancakes in a lightly greased frying pan (skillet) over moderate heat.

SOUFFLÉS

Soufflés can be either hot or cold. The hot soufflé is basically a thick sauce with the addition of separated eggs. A well-greased soufflé dish is used to allow for even rising and it should be three-quarters filled with the soufflé mixture. During cooking the soufflé should rise above the rim of the dish. A variety of flavourings can be added to the basic mixture, but too many additional ingredients can inhibit rising and result in a heavy texture. A cooked soufflé should be light, fluffy and tasty, and it must be served immediately.

By contrast, cold soufflés can be prepared well in advance. They are generally sweet and based on a mixture of cream, separated eggs and gelatine, with added flavourings. The characteristic risen appearance of a cold soufflé is obtained by securing a collar around the edge of the dish and filling it well above the rim.

To prepare a dish for a cold soufflé: place a strip of folded greaseproof (wax) paper or foil around the dish to extend about 5 cm/2 inches above the top. Secure this collar with string. Brush the dish and collar lightly with melted butter. When the soufflé mixture is added, it should extend about 2.5 cm/1 inch above the rim of the dish. Once the soufflé is set, the collar is carefully removed by running a warmed palette knife around between the soufflé and the collar.

Soufflé dish sizes: These may be described by volume or diameter. Soufflé dishes vary slightly in depth, but the following table provides a guide to size equivalents.

Diameter of dish	Volume
13 cm/5 inches	600-750 ml/1-1¼ pint
15 cm/6 inches	1-1.2 litre/1¾-2 pint
17 cm/6½ inches	1.5 litre/2½ pint
18 cm/7 inches	1.75-2 litre/3-3½ pint

FISH

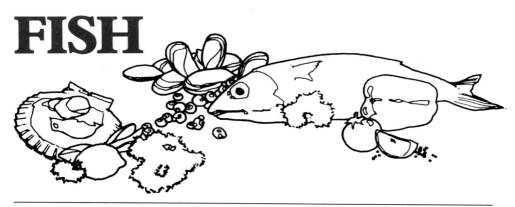

Crab Rolls

METRIC/IMPERIAL	AMERICAN
oil for deep-frying	oil for deep-frying
Crêpes:	**Crêpes:**
4 tablespoons plain flour	4 tablespoons all-purpose flour
½ teaspoon salt	½ teaspoon salt
4 tablespoons water	4 tablespoons water
4 eggs, beaten	4 eggs, beaten
Filling:	**Filling:**
2 tablespoons oil	2 tablespoons oil
1 egg, beaten	1 egg, beaten
1 spring onion, shredded	1 scallion, shredded
350 g/12 oz crab meat, flaked	¾ lb crab meat, flaked
1 tablespoon dry sherry	1 tablespoon pale dry sherry
salt and pepper	salt and pepper
1 tablespoon cornflour	1 tablespoon cornstarch
3 tablespoons water	3 tablespoons water
Flour paste:	**Flour paste:**
1 tablespoon plain flour mixed with	1 tablespoon all-purpose flour
1 tablespoon water	mixed with 1 tablespoon water

To make the crêpe batter, sift the flour and salt into a bowl, then gradually beat in the water and eggs to make a smooth batter. Using a 13 cm/15 inch frying pan (skillet), cook about 12 crêpes from the batter (see page 8) and set aside.

To make the filling, heat the oil in a pan and add the egg, spring onion (scallion) and crab meat. Stir for a few seconds, then add the sherry and salt and pepper to taste. Mix the cornflour (cornstarch) with the water and stir into the mixture. Cook, stirring, until thickened, then leave to cool.

Place 2 tablespoons of the filling on the bottom half of each crêpe, fold both sides in towards the centre and roll up like a parcel. Seal the end with the flour and water paste.

Deep-fry the rolls a few at a time until golden brown. Drain on absorbent kitchen paper and cut into diagonal pieces. Serve hot.
Serves 4

Smoked Haddock Crêpes

METRIC/IMPERIAL
8 crêpes (see page 8)
350 g/12 oz smoked haddock
1 red pepper, cored and seeded
1 green pepper, cored and seeded
25 g/1 oz butter
25 g/1 oz plain flour
150 ml/¼ pint creamy milk
few drops of Tabasco sauce
pepper

AMERICAN
8 crêpes (see page 8)
¾ lb smoked haddock
1 red pepper, cored and seeded
1 green pepper, cored and seeded
2 tablespoons butter
¼ cup all-purpose flour
⅔ cup half and half cream
few drops of Tabasco sauce
pepper

Make up the crêpes and keep warm.

Poach the haddock in water to cover for 3 to 5 minutes. Drain and reserve 150 ml/¼ pint (⅔ cup) of the liquid. Remove the skin and any bones, then flake the fish. Slice a few rings from the red pepper and set aside. Chop the remaining peppers and mix with the haddock.

Melt the butter in a saucepan, stir in the flour and cook for 1 minute. Blend in the haddock liquor and milk. Heat, stirring, until thickened. Add Tabasco and pepper to taste and cook for 1 minute.

Mix three-quarters of the sauce with the fish and divide between the crêpes. Roll up and arrange in a shallow ovenproof dish. Pour the remaining sauce over the crêpes and arrange the pepper rings on top. Place in a moderately hot oven (200°C/400°F, Gas Mark 6) for 10 to 15 minutes before serving.
Serves 4

Prawn or Shrimp Crêpes

METRIC/IMPERIAL
8 crêpes (see page 8)
Filling:
50 g/2 oz butter
50 g/2 oz plain flour
300 ml/½ pint milk
175 g/6 oz cooked shelled prawns
1 tablespoon chopped parsley
salt and pepper

AMERICAN
8 crêpes (see page 8)
Filling:
¼ cup butter
½ cup all-purpose flour
1¼ cups milk
1 cup shelled shrimp
1 tablespoon chopped parsley
salt and pepper

Make up the crêpes and keep warm.

Melt the butter in a pan, add the flour and cook for 1 minute. Blend in the milk, then heat, stirring, until thickened. Stir in the prawns (shrimp), parsley and salt and pepper to taste. Cook for 2 minutes. Divide between the crêpes, roll up and serve immediately.
Serves 4

SMOKED HADDOCK CRÊPES
(Photograph: Carmel Produce Information Service)

Cheesy Cod Rolls

METRIC/IMPERIAL	AMERICAN
8 crêpes (see page 8)	8 crêpes (see page 8)
350 g/12 oz cod fillet	¾ lb cod fillet
salt and pepper	salt and pepper
25 g/1 oz butter	2 tablespoons butter
25 g/1 oz plain flour	¼ cup all-purpose flour
300 ml/½ pint milk	1¼ cups milk
100 g/4 oz cooked peas	¾ cup cooked peas
100 g/4 oz Cheddar cheese, grated	1 cup grated cheese
25 g/1 oz fresh breadcrumbs	½ cup fresh bread crumbs
parsley sprigs to garnish	parsley sprigs to garnish

Make up the crêpes and keep warm.

Poach the cod in seasoned water to cover for 5 minutes. Drain, remove the skin and any bones, then flake the fish.

Melt the butter in a saucepan, add the flour and cook for 1 minute. Remove from the heat and gradually blend in the milk. Heat, stirring, until the sauce thickens. Add the cod and peas and cook gently for 1 to 2 minutes. Stir in three quarters of the cheese and remove from the heat.

Divide the filling between the crêpes, roll up and arrange in a shallow ovenproof dish. Mix the remaining cheese with the bread crumbs and sprinkle over the crêpes. Cover with foil and place in a moderately hot oven (190°C/375°F, Gas Mark 5) for 20 to 25 minutes. Serve hot, garnished with parsley sprigs.
Serves 4

Crab and Egg Layer

METRIC/IMPERIAL
6 crêpes (see page 8)
Filling:
25 g/1 oz butter
25 g/1 oz plain flour
300 ml/½ pint milk
1 × 185 g/6½ oz can crab meat,
  drained and flaked
few drops of Tabasco sauce
1 tablespoon chopped parsley
salt and pepper
3 hard-boiled eggs, sliced
Garnish:
1 hard-boiled egg, sliced
parsley sprigs

AMERICAN
6 crêpes (see page 8)
Filling:
2 tablespoons butter
¼ cup all-purpose flour
1¼ cups milk
1 × 6½ oz can crab meat, drained
  and flaked
few drops of Tabasco sauce
1 tablespoon chopped parsley
salt and pepper
3 hard-cooked eggs, sliced
Garnish:
1 hard-cooked egg, sliced
parsley sprigs

Make up the crêpes and keep warm.

Melt the butter in a saucepan, then add the flour and cook for
1 minute. Remove from the heat and gradually blend in the milk.
Heat, stirring, until the sauce thickens, then add the crab meat,
Tabasco, parsley, and salt and pepper to taste. Heat through gently.

Place a crêpe on a warmed serving plate and spread some crab
mixture and a few egg slices on top. Continue layering until all
filling ingredients are used, finishing with a crêpe. Garnish with egg
slices and parsley. Serve immediately.
Serves 4

Tuna and Pepper Omelets

METRIC/IMPERIAL
Filling:
1 green pepper, cored, seeded and
  sliced
1 × 200 g/7 oz can tuna fish,
  drained and flaked
100 g/4 oz cooked peas
2 tomatoes, skinned and chopped
4 tablespoons single cream
salt and pepper
Omelet mixture:
8 eggs
2 tablespoons water
25 g/1 oz butter
Garnish:
tomato slices
chopped parsley

AMERICAN
Filling:
1 green pepper, cored, seeded and
  sliced
1 × 7 oz can tuna fish, drained
  and flaked
3/4 cup cooked peas
2 tomatoes, skinned and chopped
4 tablespoons light cream
salt and pepper
Omelet mixture:
8 eggs
2 tablespoons water
2 tablespoons butter
Garnish:
tomato slices
chopped parsley

Cook the green pepper in boiling water for 2 to 3 minutes, then drain. Place in a saucepan and add the remaining filling ingredients, with salt and pepper to taste. Heat through gently while making the omelets.

Beat the eggs with the water and salt and pepper to taste. Melt a quarter of the butter in an omelet pan and pour in a quarter of the egg mixture. Cook over a moderate heat, moving the cooked mixture towards the centre with a palette knife.

When the omelet is just cooked, place a quarter of the filling on one side and fold over. Transfer to a warmed serving plate and keep warm while making 3 more omelets with the remaining ingredients. Garnish with tomato slices and parsley. Serve immediately.
Serves 4

CRAB AND EGG LAYER *(page 15)*, TUNA AND PEPPER OMELETS
(Photograph: John West Foods)

Creamy Herring Omelet

METRIC/IMPERIAL
8 eggs
2 tablespoons cream
salt and pepper
25 g/1 oz butter
1 × 200 g/7 oz can herring fillets,
  drained
50 g/2 oz lettuce, finely shredded
2 tablespoons chopped chives
4 radishes, chopped

AMERICAN
8 eggs
2 tablespoons cream
salt and pepper
2 tablespoons butter
1 × 7 oz can herring fillets,
  drained
1 cup finely shredded lettuce
2 tablespoons chopped chives
4 radishes, chopped

Beat together the eggs, cream and salt and pepper to taste. Melt the butter in a large omelet pan and pour in the egg mixture. Cook gently, moving the cooked mixture from the outside towards the centre with a palette knife. When the omelet is set, slide onto a warmed serving plate.

   Cut the herring fillets into strips and arrange over the omelet. Mix together the lettuce, chives and radishes and sprinkle over the top. Cut into quarters and serve immediately, with crusty bread.
Serves 4

Smoked Mackerel Omelets

METRIC/IMPERIAL	AMERICAN
225 g/8 oz smoked mackerel fillets	*½ lb smoked mackerel fillets*
6 eggs	*6 eggs*
4 tablespoons milk	*4 tablespoons milk*
salt and pepper	*salt and pepper*
25 g/1 oz butter	*2 tablespoons butter*
Garnish:	**Garnish:**
tomato slices	*tomato slices*
parsley sprigs	*parsley sprigs*

Remove any skin and bones from the smoked mackerel, flake coarsely and set aside.

Whisk together the eggs, milk and salt and pepper to taste. Melt a quarter of the butter in an omelet pan, and pour in a quarter of the egg mixture. Cook over a moderate heat, moving the cooked mixture towards the centre with a palette knife.

When the omelet is just set pile a quarter of the mackerel into the centre and fold over. Transfer to a serving plate and set aside while making 3 more omelets with the remaining ingredients. Garnish with the tomato slices and parsley and serve warm or cold.
Serves 4

Laird's Omelets

METRIC/IMPERIAL	AMERICAN
8 eggs	*8 eggs*
2 tablespoons water	*2 tablespoons water*
1 tablespoon chopped chives	*1 tablespoon chopped chives*
salt and pepper	*salt and pepper*
25 g/1 oz butter	*2 tablespoons butter*
100 g/4 oz smoked salmon,	*½ cup chopped smoked salmon*
chopped	*watercress sprigs to garnish*
watercress sprigs to garnish	

Whisk the eggs with the water, chives and salt and pepper to taste.

Melt a quarter of the butter in an omelet pan and pour in a quarter of the egg mixture. Cook over a moderate heat, moving the cooked mixture towards the centre with a palette knife.

When the omelet is just cooked, spoon a quarter of the smoked salmon along the middle. Fold the omelet into three and slide onto a warmed serving plate. Keep warm while making 3 more omelets with the remaining ingredients. Garnish with watercress and serve immediately.
Serves 4

Egg Foo Yung with Prawns or Shrimps

METRIC/IMPERIAL
6 eggs
½ teaspoon salt
225 g/8 oz cooked shelled prawns
  or shrimps
2 tablespoons oil

AMERICAN
6 eggs
½ teaspoon salt
½ lb cooked shelled shrimp
2 tablespoons oil

Beat the eggs with the salt and stir in the prawns or shrimps.
    Heat the oil in a large omelet pan and add the egg mixture. Cook, turning over once, until golden brown on both sides. Serve hot.
Serves 4

Smoked Haddock Soufflé Omelets

METRIC/IMPERIAL
350 g/12 oz smoked haddock
50 g/2 oz butter
1 tablespoon chopped parsley
8 eggs, separated
salt and pepper
chopped parsley to garnish

AMERICAN
¾ lb smoked haddock
¼ cup butter
1 tablespoon chopped parsley
8 eggs, separated
salt and pepper
chopped parsley to garnish

Poach the haddock in water for 3 to 5 minutes. Drain well, remove the skin and any bones, and then flake. Melt half of the butter in a small pan and add the fish and parsley. Keep warm over a low heat.
    Beat the yolks with salt and pepper to taste. Whisk the egg whites until just stiff and fold into the yolk mixture, with the fish mixture. Melt a quarter of the remaining butter in an omelet pan and add a quarter of the egg mixture. Cook, without moving, until the omelet is set and a pale golden brown underneath. Place the pan under a hot grill (broiler) for 30 seconds to 1 minute until the top is just cooked. Fold the omelet in half and slide onto a warmed serving plate.
    Keep warm while making 3 more omelets with the remaining ingredients. Garnish with parsley and serve immediately, with hot buttered toast.
Serves 4

Kipper Soufflé

METRIC/IMPERIAL
50 g/2 oz butter, softened
8 slices French bread,
  0.5 cm/¼ inch thick
Soufflé mixture:
100 g/4 oz kipper fillets
150 ml/¼ pint milk
 (approximately)
25 g/1 oz butter
25 g/1 oz plain flour
3 eggs, separated
50 g/2 oz Leicester cheese, grated
salt and pepper

AMERICAN
¼ cup softened butter
8 slices French bread, ¼ inch thick
Soufflé mixture:
¼ lb kipper fillets
⅔ cup milk (approximately)
2 tablespoons butter
¼ cup all-purpose flour
3 eggs, separated
½ cup grated cheese
salt and pepper

Spread the softened butter over both sides of the bread and use to line the sides of a 900 ml/1½ pint soufflé dish.

Poach the kippers in the milk for 5 minutes, then drain, reserving the liquid. Make this up to 150 ml/¼ pint (⅔ cup) with milk, if necessary. Mash the kipper fillets and set aside.

Melt the butter in a saucepan, then stir in the flour and cook for 1 minute. Remove from the heat and gradually blend in the milk. Heat, stirring, until the mixture comes to the boil. Cool slightly, then beat in the egg yolks, kippers and cheese. Add salt and pepper to taste.

Whisk the egg whites until stiff and fold into the mixture, using a metal spoon. Pour into the soufflé dish, taking care not to disturb the bread. Cook in a moderately hot oven (200°C/400°F, Gas Mark 6) for 30 to 35 minutes, until well risen and golden brown. Serve immediately.
Serves 4

Haddock and Cheese Soufflé

METRIC/IMPERIAL
175 g/6 oz smoked haddock
250 ml/8 fl oz milk
 (approximately)
25 g/1 oz butter
25 g/1 oz plain flour
¾ teaspoon dry mustard
¾ teaspoon dried marjoram
3 eggs, separated
100 g/4 oz Cheddar cheese, grated
salt and pepper

AMERICAN
6 oz smoked haddock
1 cup milk (approximately)
2 tablespoons butter
¼ cup all-purpose flour
¾ teaspoon dry mustard
¾ teaspoon dried marjoram
3 eggs, separated
1 cup grated cheese
salt and pepper

Poach the haddock in the milk for 10 minutes, then drain, reserving the liquid. Make this up to 250 ml/8 fl oz (1 cup) with milk, if necessary. Flake the haddock and set aside.

Melt the butter in a large saucepan, then stir in the flour, mustard and marjoram. Cook for 1 minute. Remove from the heat and gradually blend in the fish liquor. Bring to the boil, stirring. Remove from the heat, cool slightly and beat in the egg yolks, smoked haddock, cheese and salt and pepper to taste.

Whisk the egg whites until stiff, then fold into the fish mixture, using a metal spoon. Pour into a greased 750 ml/1¼ pint soufflé dish. Cook in a moderately hot oven (190°C/375°F, Gas Mark 5) for about 40 minutes or until well risen and golden brown. Serve immediately.
Serves 4

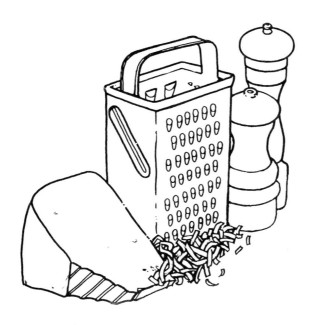

MEAT AND POULTRY

Bacon and Soured Cream Crêpes with Melon

METRIC/IMPERIAL
8 crêpes (see page 8)
Filling:
225 g/8 oz cooked bacon, chopped
300 ml/1/2 pint soured cream
1 clove garlic, crushed
2 tablespoons chopped chives
salt and pepper
Garnish:
100 g/4 oz Cheddar cheese, grated
1 melon, halved and deseeded
parsley sprig

AMERICAN
8 crêpes (see page 8)
Filling:
1 cup chopped cooked bacon
1 1/4 cups sour cream
1 clove garlic, minced
2 tablespoons chopped chives
salt and pepper
Garnish:
1 cup grated Cheddar cheese
1 melon, halved and pips removed
parsley sprig

Make up the crêpes and keep warm.

Combine the bacon, cream, garlic and chives with salt and pepper to taste; mix well.

Divide the mixture between the crêpes, roll up and arrange in a shallow ovenproof dish. Sprinkle with the cheese, cover with foil and place in a moderately hot oven (190°C/375°F, Gas Mark 5) for 20 minutes.

Using a melon baller, scoop the melon flesh into balls. Before serving, garnish the crêpes with the melon and parsley. Serve hot.
Serves 4

BACON AND SOURED CREAM CRÊPES WITH MELON
(Photograph: Carmel Produce Information Service)

Curried Chicken Crêpes

METRIC/IMPERIAL
8 crêpes (see page 8)
Filling:
15 g/½ oz margarine
1 small onion, finely chopped
350 g/12 oz cooked chicken,
  chopped
1 tablespoon mango chutney
2 teaspoons lemon juice
1 tablespoon curry paste
150 ml/¼ pint soured cream
salt and pepper
Garnish:
parsley sprigs
lemon slices

AMERICAN
8 crêpes (see page 8)
Filling:
1 tablespoon margarine
1 small onion, finely chopped
1½ cups chopped cooked chicken
1 tablespoon mango chutney
2 teaspoons lemon juice
1 tablespoon curry paste
⅔ cup sour cream
salt and pepper
Garnish:
parsley sprigs
lemon slices

Make up the crêpes and keep warm.

Melt the margarine in a pan and fry the onion for 3 to 4 minutes. Stir in the remaining filling ingredients and simmer for 5 minutes or until thoroughly heated through; do not boil.

Divide the mixture between the hot crêpes and roll up. Arrange on a hot serving dish and garnish with parsley and lemon slices. Serve immediately with a selection of the following side dishes: tomato slices in vinaigrette dressing; cucumber slices in natural (unflavored) yogurt; banana slices tossed in lemon juice; salted peanuts; mango chutney.
Serves 4

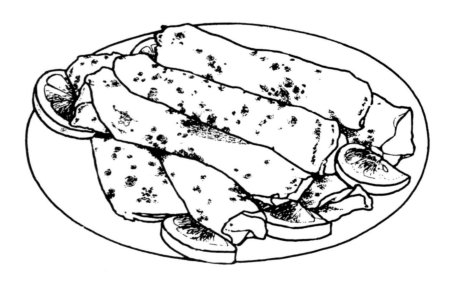

Tangy Chicken Crêpes

METRIC/IMPERIAL	AMERICAN
8 crêpes (see page 8)	*8 crêpes (see page 8)*
Filling:	**Filling:**
25 g/1 oz butter	*2 tablespoons butter*
1 onion, chopped	*1 onion, chopped*
2 oranges	*2 oranges*
4 tablespoons white wine	*4 tablespoons white wine*
150 ml/¼ pint chicken stock	*⅔ cup chicken stock*
salt and pepper	*salt and pepper*
225 g/8 oz cooked chicken, diced	*1 cup diced cooked chicken*
2 teaspoons cornflour	*2 teaspoons cornstarch*
2 tablespoons water	*2 tablespoons water*
Garnish:	**Garnish:**
chopped parsley	*chopped parsley*

Make up the crêpes and keep warm.

Melt the butter in a saucepan, add the onion and fry until soft. Add the grated rind of 1 orange, the juice from 2 oranges, wine, stock, and salt and pepper to taste. Bring to the boil, then cover and simmer for 5 minutes. Add the chicken and continue to cook for 5 minutes.

Blend the cornflour (cornstarch) with the water and add to the pan. Heat, stirring, until the mixture thickens. Cook, stirring, for 2 minutes. Check the seasoning.

Divide the mixture between the crêpes, roll up and arrange in a shallow ovenproof dish. Cover with foil and place in a moderate oven (180°C/350°F, Gas Mark 4) for 20 minutes.

Garnish with parsley and serve immediately.

Serves 4

Chinese Chicken Crêpes:

Follow the above recipe, omitting the oranges and wine. Fry 50 g/2 oz (½ cup) sliced mushrooms and 2 sliced carrots with the onion. Add 2 tablespoons water with the stock. Stir in 175 g/6 oz (3 cups) fresh or canned beansprouts with the chicken. Finish as above.

Lamb and Kidney Crêpes

METRIC/IMPERIAL
8 crêpes (see page 8)
Filling:
25 g/1 oz butter
350 g/12 oz lambs' kidneys, cored
  and chopped
2 tablespoons plain flour
300 ml/½ pint beef stock
100 g/4 oz cooked lamb, chopped
salt and pepper
chopped parsley to garnish

AMERICAN
8 crêpes (see page 8)
Filling:
2 tablespoons butter
¾ lb lamb kidneys, cored and
  chopped
2 tablespoons all-purpose flour
1¼ cups beef stock
½ cup chopped cooked lamb
salt and pepper
chopped parsley to garnish

Make up the crêpes and keep warm.

Melt the butter in a saucepan, add the kidneys and fry for 2 to 3 minutes. Stir in the flour and cook for 1 minute. Remove from the heat, blend in the stock, then heat, stirring, until thickened. Add the lamb and salt and pepper to taste. Simmer, stirring, for 2 minutes.

Using a slotted spoon, divide the kidneys between the crêpes. Spoon a little of the sauce over, roll up and arrange in a warmed serving dish. Spoon the remaining sauce over the crêpes, garnish with parsley and serve immediately.
Serves 4

Party Crêpe Kebabs

METRIC/IMPERIAL
300 ml/½ pint crêpe batter (see
  page 8)
500 g/1 lb cooked lamb, cubed
4 tablespoons chutney, warmed

AMERICAN
1¼ cups crêpe batter (see page 8)
2 cups diced cooked lamb
4 tablespoons chutney, warmed

Using a lightly oiled frying pan (skillet) and 1 tablespoon of the batter for each one, cook 25 miniature crêpes (see page 8). Keep the crêpes warm.

Brush the cubes of lamb with the chutney and place one in the centre of each crêpe. Wrap up to form neat parcels and secure with cocktail sticks (toothpicks). Serve hot, with a selection of salads.
Makes 25 kebabs

LAMB AND KIDNEY CRÊPES, PARTY CRÊPE KEBABS
(Photograph: New Zealand Lamb Information Bureau)

Cheesy Beef Crêpes

METRIC/IMPERIAL
8 crêpes (see page 8)
Filling:
1 tablespoon oil
1 onion, chopped
1 clove garlic, crushed
225 g/8 oz minced beef
2 tablespoons plain flour
150 ml/¼ pint beef stock
2-3 tablespoons tomato purée
100 g/4 oz button mushrooms,
 sliced
salt and pepper
Sauce:
25 g/1 oz butter
25 g/1 oz plain flour
300 ml/½ pint milk
75 g/3 oz cheese, grated

AMERICAN
8 crêpes (see page 8)
Filling:
1 tablespoon oil
1 onion, chopped
1 clove garlic, minced
1 cup ground beef
2 tablespoons all-purpose flour
⅔ cup beef stock
2-3 tablespoons tomato paste
1 cup sliced button mushrooms
salt and pepper
Sauce:
2 tablespoons butter
¼ cup all-purpose flour
1 ¼ cups milk
¾ cup grated cheese

Make up the crêpes and keep warm.

Heat the oil in a pan, add the onion and garlic and fry until soft. Add the beef and cook for 3 to 4 minutes, then stir in the flour and cook for 1 minute. Add the stock, tomato purée (paste), mushrooms and salt and pepper to taste. Bring to the boil, then cover and simmer for 30 minutes.

To make the sauce, melt the butter in a saucepan, add the flour and cook for 1 minute. Remove from the heat and gradually blend in the milk, stirring, until the sauce thickens, then continue to cook for 1 minute. Stir in two thirds of the cheese and salt and pepper to taste.

Divide the filling between the crêpes, roll up and arrange on a heatproof serving dish. Pour the sauce over the crêpes and sprinkle with the remaining cheese. Place under a hot grill (broiler) for 2 to 3 minutes until golden brown. Serve immediately.
Serves 4

Mexican Crêpes
Prepare the crêpes and filling as above, omitting the mushrooms and adding one 425 g/15 oz can drained red kidney beans, ½ teaspoon ground chilli, 2 teaspoons creamed horseradish, a pinch of ground mace and 1 tablespoon chopped parsley to the filling with the stock. Omit the cheese sauce. Sprinkle the stuffed crêpes with grated Parmesan cheese and serve immediately.

Ham and Mushroom Omelet Layer

METRIC/IMPERIAL	AMERICAN
Filling:	**Filling:**
3 tablespoons oil	3 tablespoons oil
1 green pepper, cored, seeded and chopped	1 green pepper, cored, seeded and chopped
1 clove garlic, crushed	1 clove garlic, minced
100 g/4 oz ham, minced	½ cup ground ham
175 g/6 oz mushrooms, sliced	1½ cups sliced mushrooms
1 dessert apple, peeled, cored and sliced	1 dessert apple, peeled, cored and sliced
1 tablespoon chopped chives	1 tablespoon chopped chives
salt and pepper	salt and pepper
Sauce:	**Sauce:**
750 g/1½ lb tomatoes, skinned	1½ lb tomatoes, skinned
25 g/1 oz butter	2 tablespoons butter
1 small onion, chopped	1 small onion, chopped
1 clove garlic, crushed	1 clove garlic, minced
25 g/1 oz plain flour	¼ cup all-purpose flour
5 tablespoons water	5 tablespoons water
Omelets:	**Omelets:**
6 eggs	6 eggs
1 tablespoon water	1 tablespoon water
40 g/1½ oz butter	3 tablespoons butter
Garnish:	**Garnish:**
chopped parsley	chopped parsley

To make the ham filling, heat 1 tablespoon oil in a pan. Add the pepper and garlic and cook until soft. Add the ham and heat through.

Heat the remaining oil in another pan, add the mushrooms and apple and cook until soft. Add the chives and salt and pepper to taste.

To make the sauce, purée the tomatoes in an electric blender or rub through a sieve. Melt the butter in a pan and fry the onion and garlic until soft. Add the flour and cook, stirring, for 1 minute. Add the tomato pulp, water and salt and pepper to taste. Bring to the boil, cover and simmer for 10 minutes.

Whisk together the eggs, water and salt and pepper to taste. Melt a third of the butter in an omelet pan, add one third of the egg mixture and cook over a medium heat; keep warm while making 2 more omelets with the remaining ingredients.

Place one omelet on a warmed serving dish and cover with the ham filling. Place another omelet on top and cover with the mushroom filling. Top with the third omelet, pour the tomato sauce over and sprinkle with parsley. Serve immediately, cut into wedges.
Serves 4

Hawaiian Omelets

METRIC/IMPERIAL
Filling:
50 g/2 oz butter
175 g/6 oz mushrooms, chopped
100 g/4 oz ham, diced
100 g/4 oz canned pineapple,
 chopped
Omelets:
8 eggs
2 tablespoons water
salt and pepper
50 g/2 oz butter

AMERICAN
Filling:
¼ cup butter
1½ cups chopped mushrooms
½ cup finely chopped ham
2 rings canned pineapple, chopped
Omelets:
8 eggs
2 tablespoons water
salt and pepper
¼ cup butter

Melt the butter in a saucepan, add the mushrooms, ham and pineapple and sauté for 3 to 4 minutes.

Whisk together the eggs, water and salt and pepper to taste. Melt a quarter of the butter in an omelet pan. Add a quarter of the egg mixture and cook over a medium heat, moving the cooked mixture towards the centre with a palette knife.

When the omelet is set, spoon over a quarter of the filling. Fold in half, slide onto a warmed serving plate, and keep warm while making 3 more omelets with the remaining ingredients. Serve hot.
Serves 4

New Zealand Omelet

METRIC/IMPERIAL
2 tablespoons oil
1 large onion, sliced into rings
225 g/8 oz cooked lamb, diced
2 tomatoes, skinned and chopped
4 eggs
1 teaspoon mint sauce
salt and pepper

AMERICAN
2 tablespoons oil
1 large onion, sliced into rings
1 cup finely chopped cooked lamb
2 tomatoes, skinned and chopped
4 eggs
1 teaspoon mint sauce
salt and pepper

Heat the oil in a large frying pan (skillet). Add the onion, lamb and tomatoes and cook over a moderate heat until the onion is soft.

Beat the eggs with the mint sauce and salt and pepper to taste. Add to the frying pan (skillet) and cook over a low heat until the omelet is firm and golden underneath. Place under a hot grill (broiler) for 1 to 2 minutes. Cut into wedges and serve immediately, with a tossed salad.
Serves 4

HAM AND MUSHROOM OMELET LAYER *(page 31)*,
HAWAIIAN OMELETS
(Photograph: Mushroom Growers' Association)

Chicken Liver Omelet

METRIC/IMPERIAL
Filling:
100 g/4 oz chicken livers
1 tablespoon oil
1 small onion, finely chopped
1 tablespoon dry sherry
150 ml/¼ pint chicken stock
1 teaspoon tomato purée
1 clove garlic, crushed
salt and pepper
Omelet:
8 eggs
1 tablespoon single cream
25 g/1 oz butter
Garnish:
chopped parsley

AMERICAN
Filling:
¼ lb chicken livers
1 tablespoon oil
1 small onion, finely chopped
1 tablespoon pale dry sherry
⅔ cup chicken stock
1 teaspoon tomato paste
1 clove garlic, minced
salt and pepper
Omelet:
8 eggs
1 tablespoon light cream
2 tablespoons butter
Garnish:
chopped parsley

Cut the livers into 1 cm/½ inch strips, then rinse and drain on
absorbent kitchen paper. Heat the oil in a pan, add the livers and
cook, stirring, for 30 seconds. Add the onion and continue to cook
for 1 minute. Remove the livers and onion from the pan, using a
slotted spoon, and set aside.

Pour the sherry and stock into the pan and boil until reduced by
about half. Stir in the tomato purée (paste), garlic and salt and pepper
to taste. Return the livers and onion to the pan and heat through
without boiling.

Whisk together the eggs and cream with salt and pepper to taste.
Heat the butter in a large frying pan (skillet) and, when sizzling, pour
in the eggs. Cook over a moderate heat, shaking the pan and stirring
with a fork. When the mixture resembles a lightly scrambled egg,
stop mixing and leave to cook until the omelet is set and golden
brown underneath.

Slide the omelet onto a large warmed serving plate. Spread the
chicken liver mixture over the top, fold over and sprinkle with
parsley. Serve hot, cut into wedges.
Serves 4

Tangy Kidney Omelets

METRIC/IMPERIAL
Filling:
40 g/1 ½ oz butter
1 teaspoon yeast extract
8 lambs' kidneys, skinned, cored
  and sliced
Omelets:
8 eggs
8 tablespoons milk
salt and pepper
50 g/2 oz butter
Garnish:
tomato slices
parsley sprigs

AMERICAN
Filling:
3 tablespoons butter
1 teaspoon Brewers' yeast
8 lamb kidneys, skinned, cored and
  sliced
Omelets:
8 eggs
8 tablespoons milk
salt and pepper
¼ cup butter
Garnish:
tomato slices
parsley sprigs

Melt the butter in a pan, add the yeast extract (Brewers' yeast) and kidneys and cook until tender. Keep warm while making the omelets.

Whisk together the eggs, milk and salt and pepper to taste. Melt a quarter of the butter in an omelet pan, then add a quarter of the egg mixture. Cook over a medium heat, moving the cooked mixture towards the centre with a palette knife.

When the omelet is cooked, place a quarter of the kidneys on one half. Fold over, slide onto a warmed serving plate and keep warm while making 3 more omelets with the remaining ingredients. Serve immediately, garnished with tomato and parsley.
Serves 4

Continental Meat Soufflé

METRIC/IMPERIAL	AMERICAN
25 g/1 oz butter	2 tablespoons butter
25 g/1 oz plain flour	¼ cup all-purpose flour
250 ml/8 fl oz milk	1 cup milk
1 × 100 g/4 oz chub pack of ham and tongue pâté, mashed	1 × ¼ lb package ham and tongue pâté, mashed
1 teaspoon dry mustard	1 teaspoon dry mustard
salt and pepper	salt and pepper
3 eggs, separated	3 eggs, separated
100 g/4 oz mushrooms, sliced	1 cup sliced mushrooms
300 ml/½ pint boiling water	1¼ cups boiling water
50 g/2 oz garlic sausage, chopped	¼ cup chopped garlic sausage
50 g/2 oz Danish salami, chopped	¼ cup chopped Danish salami
25 g/1 oz Cheddar cheese, grated	¼ cup grated Cheddar cheese

Melt the butter in a saucepan, stir in the flour and cook for 1 minute. Remove from the heat and gradually blend in the milk. Heat, stirring, until the sauce thickens and continue to cook for 1 minute. Stir in the pâté, mustard and salt and pepper to taste. Beat in the egg yolks.

Place the mushrooms in a bowl and pour over the boiling water. Leave for 1 minute, then drain and mix with the garlic sausage and salami.

Whisk the egg whites until stiff and fold into the soufflé mixture. Place alternate layers of this and the meat mixture in a greased 1.2 litre/2 pint soufflé dish, finishing with a layer of soufflé mixture.

Sprinkle with the cheese and place in a moderate oven (180°C/350°F, Gas Mark 4) for 30 minutes until well risen and golden. Serve immediately, with salad.
Serves 4

CONTINENTAL MEAT SOUFFLÉ
(Photograph: Corning Ltd – Manufacturers of Pyrex)

Lamb and Spinach Soufflé

METRIC/IMPERIAL
50 g/2 oz butter
50 g/2 oz plain flour
300 ml/½ pint milk
225 g/8 oz cooked lamb, diced
50 g/2 oz cooked spinach, diced
3 eggs, separated
salt and pepper

AMERICAN
¼ cup butter
½ cup all-purpose flour
1¼ cups milk
1 cup finely chopped cooked lamb
¼ cup chopped cooked spinach
3 eggs, separated
salt and pepper

Melt the butter in a saucepan, stir in the flour and cook for 1 minute.
Remove from the heat and gradually blend in the milk. Heat,
stirring, until the sauce thickens. Cool slightly, then add the lamb,
spinach, egg yolks and salt and pepper to taste. Mix thoroughly.

Whisk the egg whites until stiff and fold into the lamb mixture.
Turn into a greased 1.2 litre/2 pint soufflé dish and place in a
moderately hot oven (190°C/375°F, Gas Mark 5) for 35 to 40 minutes
until well risen and golden brown. Serve immediately, with salad or
green vegetables.
Serves 4

Chicken and Orange Soufflé

METRIC/IMPERIAL
25 g/1 oz butter
25 g/1 oz plain flour
300 ml/½ pint chicken stock
3 egg yolks
175 g/6 oz cooked chicken, minced
grated rind of 1 orange
salt and pepper
4 egg whites

AMERICAN
2 tablespoons butter
¼ cup all-purpose flour
1¼ cups chicken stock
3 egg yolks
¾ cup ground cooked chicken
grated rind of 1 orange
salt and pepper
4 egg whites

Melt the butter in a saucepan, stir in the flour and cook for 1 minute.
Remove from the heat and gradually blend in the chicken stock.
Heat, stirring, until the sauce thickens. Cool slightly, then beat in the
egg yolks.

Stir in the chicken, orange rind and salt and pepper to taste. Whisk
the egg whites until stiff and fold into the soufflé mixture evenly.
Turn into a greased 1.2 litre/2 pint soufflé dish. Place in a moderately
hot oven (190°C/375°F, Gas Mark 5) for 30 to 40 minutes until well
risen and golden brown. Serve immediately.
Serves 4

Cold Chicken Soufflé

METRIC/IMPERIAL
40 g/1½ oz butter
25 g/1 oz plain flour
300 ml/½ pint chicken stock
2 eggs, separated
3 tablespoons water
1 tablespoon gelatine
2 tablespoons dry sherry
225 g/8 oz cooked chicken, minced
25 g/1 oz ham, minced
2 hard-boiled eggs, chopped
150 ml/¼ pint double cream,
 lightly whipped
salt and pepper
Garnish:
1 hard-boiled egg, sliced
chopped parsley

AMERICAN
3 tablespoons butter
¼ cup all-purpose flour
1¼ cups chicken stock
2 eggs, separated
3 tablespoons water
1 envelope gelatin
2 tablespoons pale dry sherry
1 cup ground cooked chicken
2 tablespoons ground ham
2 hard-cooked eggs, chopped
⅔ cup heavy cream, lightly
 whipped
salt and pepper
Garnish:
1 hard-cooked egg, sliced
chopped parsley

Prepare a 1.2 litre/2 pint soufflé dish for making a cold soufflé
(see page 9).

Melt the butter in a saucepan, stir in the flour and cook for
1 minute. Remove from the heat and gradually blend in the stock.
Heat, stirring, until the sauce thickens. Simmer, stirring, for
1 minute. Cool slightly, then beat in the egg yolks.

Put the water in a small bowl and sprinkle over the gelatine. Place
over a pan of hot water and stir until the gelatine is dissolved. Stir in
the sherry.

Stir the gelatine, chicken, ham and hard-boiled (hard-cooked) eggs
into the sauce, then fold in the cream. Add salt and pepper to taste.
Whisk the egg whites until stiff and fold into the soufflé mixture
evenly. Turn into the soufflé dish and leave in a cool place until set.

Carefully remove the collar from the dish and garnish the soufflé
with egg slices and parsley before serving.
Serves 4

VEGETARIAN DISHES

Slimmer's Salad Crêpe Layer

METRIC/IMPERIAL	AMERICAN
8 crêpes (see page 8)	8 crêpes (see page 8)
Filling:	**Filling:**
225 g/8 oz cottage cheese	1 cup curd cheese
3 spring onions, chopped	3 scallions, chopped
1 tablespoon rosehip syrup	1 tablespoon rosehip syrup
salt and pepper	salt and pepper
few lettuce leaves	few lettuce leaves
2 tomatoes, sliced	2 tomatoes, sliced
1 bunch watercress	1 bunch watercress
¼ cucumber, sliced	¼ cucumber, sliced
2 cooked beetroots, sliced	2 cooked beets, sliced
6 radishes, sliced	6 radishes, sliced
Garnish:	**Garnish:**
tomato slices	tomato slices
watercress	watercress

Make up the crêpes and allow to cool.

Place the cheese, spring onions (scallions) and syrup in a bowl.
Season liberally with salt and pepper and mix well.

Place one crêpe on a serving plate and cover with half the lettuce
and tomato. Season and place another crêpe on top. Spread with half
the cheese mixture and cover with another crêpe. Arrange half the
watercress and cucumber over the top, season and add another crêpe,
then cover with half the beetroot (beet) and radishes.

Repeat each layer once more, finishing with a crêpe, and garnish
with tomato and watercress. Serve cold, cut into wedges.
Serves 4

SLIMMER'S SALAD CRÊPE LAYER
(Photograph: Delrosa)

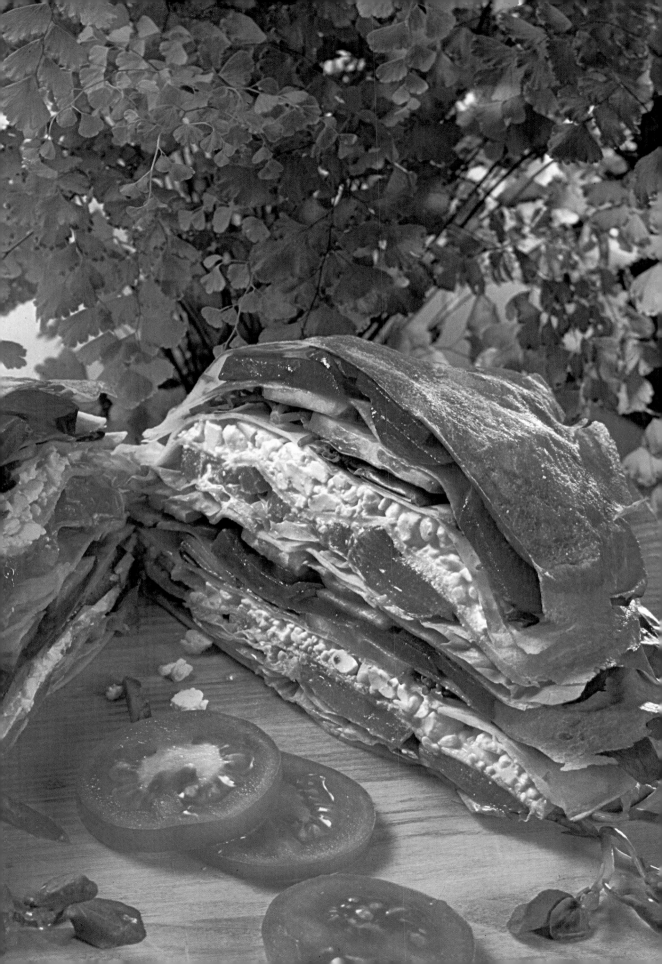

Ratatouille Crêpes

METRIC/IMPERIAL
8 crêpes (see page 8)
Filling:
3 tablespoons oil
¼ teaspoon fennel seed
1 onion, chopped
2 cloves garlic, crushed
1 large aubergine, diced
1 green pepper, cored, seeded and
  sliced
2 courgettes, diced
4 tomatoes, skinned and chopped
2 teaspoons sugar
salt and pepper
Sauce:
25 g/1 oz butter
25 g/1 oz plain flour
300 ml/½ pint milk
75 g/3 oz Cheddar cheese, grated
Garnish:
chopped parsley

AMERICAN
8 crêpes (see page 8)
Filling:
3 tablespoons oil
¼ teaspoon fennel seed
1 onion, chopped
2 cloves garlic, minced
1 large eggplant, diced
1 green pepper, cored, seeded and
  sliced
2 zucchini, diced
4 tomatoes, skinned and chopped
2 teaspoons sugar
salt and pepper
Sauce:
2 tablespoons butter
¼ cup all-purpose flour
1¼ cups milk
¾ cup grated Cheddar cheese
Garnish:
chopped parsley

Make up the crêpes and keep warm.
   To make the filling, heat the oil in a large saucepan and sauté the fennel seed for 1 minute. Add the onion, garlic and aubergine (eggplant) and cook for 4 to 5 minutes. Add the green pepper, courgettes (zucchini), tomatoes, sugar and salt and pepper to taste. Cover and cook over a low heat for 20 to 25 minutes.
   To make the sauce, heat the butter in a saucepan, add the flour and cook for 1 minute. Remove from the heat and gradually blend in the milk. Heat, stirring, until the sauce thickens, then add the cheese and salt and pepper to taste.
   Divide the ratatouille mixture between the crêpes and roll up. Arrange on a warmed serving dish and pour the cheese sauce over the crêpes. Sprinkle with parsley and serve immediately.
Serves 4

Mushroom and Bean Crêpes:
Prepare the crêpes and cheese sauce as above. For the filling, sauté 1 chopped onion, 1 crushed (minced) garlic clove, 100 g/4 oz (½ cup) chopped French (green) beans and 100 g/4 oz (1 cup) chopped mushrooms in 1 tablespoon oil until soft. Mix the vegetables with half the sauce and use to stuff the crêpes. Pour the remaining sauce over the top. Serve immediately, garnished with tomato slices.

Savoury Florentine Layer

METRIC/IMPERIAL
8 crêpes (see page 8)
Tomato filling:
1 × 225 g/8 oz can tomatoes
15 g/½ oz butter
1 onion, chopped
1 tablespoon plain flour
100 g/4 oz cheese, grated
¼ teaspoon dried oregano
salt and pepper
Spinach filling:
1 × 225 g/8 oz packet frozen
 spinach
15 g/½ oz butter
150 ml/¼ pint milk
1 tablespoon cornflour
grated nutmeg
Garnish:
watercress sprigs

AMERICAN
8 crêpes (see page 8)
Tomato filling:
1 × ½ lb can tomatoes
1 tablespoon butter
1 onion, chopped
1 tablespoon all-purpose flour
1 cup grated cheese
¼ teaspoon dried oregano
salt and pepper
Spinach filling:
1 × ½ lb package frozen spinach
1 tablespoon butter
⅔ cup milk
1 tablespoon cornstarch
grated nutmeg
Garnish:
watercress sprigs

Make up the crêpes and keep warm.

To make the tomato filling, purée the tomatoes in an electric blender or press through a sieve. Melt the butter in a saucepan, add the onion and cook gently until soft. Add the flour and cook for 1 minute. Gradually blend in the tomato pulp and heat, stirring, until the mixture thickens. Add the cheese, oregano and salt and pepper to taste; heat gently for 1 minute.

To make the spinach filling, place the spinach in a saucepan with the butter, cover and cook gently until thawed. Blend 2 tablespoons milk with the cornflour (cornstarch) and set aside. Add the remaining milk to the spinach with nutmeg and salt and pepper to taste. Bring to the boil and simmer for 2 minutes. Stir in the blended cornflour (cornstarch) and heat, stirring, until the mixture thickens.

Layer the crêpes on a warmed serving plate with alternate layers of tomato and spinach filling. Garnish with watercress and serve hot, cut into wedges.
Serves 4

Mexicorn Crêpe Medley

METRIC/IMPERIAL
8 crêpes (see page 8)
Filling:
15 g/½ oz butter
2 celery sticks, chopped
2 tablespoons plain flour
150 ml/¼ pint milk
1 × 350 g/12 oz can Mexicorn,
  drained
2 tomatoes, skinned and chopped
50 g/2 oz walnuts, chopped
1 tablespoon chopped chives
salt and pepper
100 g/4 oz Cheddar cheese, grated
Garnish:
watercress sprigs

AMERICAN
8 crêpes (see page 8)
Filling:
1 tablespoon butter
2 celery stalks, chopped
2 tablespoons all-purpose flour
⅔ cup milk
1 × 12 oz can Mexicorn, drained
2 tomatoes, skinned and chopped
½ cup chopped walnuts
1 tablespoon chopped chives
salt and pepper
1 cup grated Cheddar cheese
Garnish:
watercress sprigs

Make up the crêpes and keep warm.

Melt the butter in a saucepan, add the celery and sauté for 5 minutes. Stir in the flour and cook, stirring, for 1 minute. Gradually blend in the milk and cook, stirring, until thickened. Add the remaining ingredients, except the cheese, with salt and pepper to taste. Stir over low heat until the mixture is thoroughly heated through. Remove from the heat and stir in the cheese.

Divide the mixture between the crêpes and roll up. Arrange in a warmed shallow serving dish. Garnish with watercress and serve immediately.
Serves 4

Asparagus Omelet with Soured Cream

METRIC/IMPERIAL	AMERICAN
6 eggs	6 eggs
1 tablespoon water	1 tablespoon water
salt and pepper	salt and pepper
½ teaspoon chopped mixed herbs	½ teaspoon chopped mixed herbs
1 × 425 g/15 oz can asparagus spears, drained	1 × 15 oz can asparagus spears, drained
15 g/½ oz butter	1 tablespoon butter
pinch of garlic salt	pinch of garlic salt
4 tablespoons soured cream	4 tablespoons sour cream
25 g/1 oz grated Parmesan cheese	¼ cup grated Parmesan cheese

Beat together the eggs, water, salt, pepper and herbs. Chop half the asparagus and add to the eggs. Melt the butter in a large frying pan (skillet). Add the egg mixture and cook over a medium heat, drawing the cooked mixture towards the centre.

When the omelet begins to set, mix the garlic salt with the soured cream and spoon over the top. Arrange the remaining asparagus over the cream and top with the cheese. Place under a hot grill (broiler) for 1 to 2 minutes. Cut into wedges and serve immediately.
Serves 4

Dutch Soufflé Omelets

METRIC/IMPERIAL	AMERICAN
8 eggs, separated	8 eggs, separated
8 tablespoons milk	8 tablespoons milk
225 g/8 oz Gouda cheese, grated	2 cups grated Gouda cheese
8 rusks, crushed	8 zweiback crackers, crushed
salt and pepper	salt and pepper
25 g/1 oz butter	2 tablespoons butter

Beat the egg yolks and add the milk, cheese, crushed rusks (zweiback crackers) and salt and pepper to taste. Whisk the egg whites until stiff and fold into the cheese mixture.

Melt a quarter of the butter in an omelet pan and add a quarter of the mixture. Cook without moving until the omelet is set and golden underneath. Place under a hot grill (broiler) for 30 seconds to 1 minute. Fold in half and slide onto a warmed serving plate. Keep warm while making 3 more omelets with the remaining ingredients. Serve immediately.
Serves 4

Crunchy Mushroom Omelets

METRIC/IMPERIAL
4 slices wholemeal bread
50 g/2 oz butter
1 large onion, sliced
175 g/6 oz mushrooms, sliced
8 eggs
salt and pepper
lettuce to garnish

AMERICAN
4 slices wholewheat bread
¼ cup butter
1 large onion, sliced
1½ cups sliced mushrooms
8 eggs
salt and pepper
lettuce to garnish

Remove the crusts from the bread and cut the slices into 1 cm/½ inch squares. Melt a quarter of the butter in an omelet pan and add a quarter of the bread and onion. Fry for 5 to 6 minutes until the bread is golden brown, then add a quarter of the mushrooms and continue cooking for 1 minute.

Beat 2 eggs with salt and pepper to taste and add to the pan. Cook over a moderate heat, moving the cooked mixture towards the centre with a palette knife. Cover the pan and continue cooking until the omelet is golden brown underneath. Slide onto a warmed serving plate and keep hot while making 3 more omelets with the remaining ingredients. Serve hot, garnished with lettuce.
Serves 4

Vegetable Tortilla

METRIC/IMPERIAL
25 g/1 oz margarine
1 large onion, sliced
1 teaspoon yeast extract
4 eggs
3 tablespoons water
pepper
225 g/8 oz cooked potato, diced
100 g/4 oz green beans, cooked

AMERICAN
2 tablespoons margarine
1½ cups sliced onion
1 teaspoon Brewers' yeast
4 eggs
3 tablespoons water
pepper
1¼ cups cooked, diced potato
½ cup cooked green beans

Melt the margarine in a 20 cm/8 inch omelet pan, add the onion and cook until soft. Stir in the yeast extract (Brewers' yeast).

Beat together the eggs, water and pepper to taste, pour onto the onion and stir well. Add the potato and beans. Cook the mixture gently, stirring occasionally, until the egg is firm.

Place under a hot grill (broiler) for 2 to 3 minutes until the omelet is firm and golden on top. Cut into wedges and serve, hot or cold, with a salad and crusty bread.
Serves 3 to 4

Cheese Soufflé

METRIC/IMPERIAL	AMERICAN
40 g/1½ oz butter	3 tablespoons butter
2 tablespoons plain flour	2 tablespoons all-purpose flour
300 ml/½ pint milk	1¼ cups milk
4 eggs, separated	4 eggs, separated
100 g/4 oz Cheddar cheese, grated	1 cup grated Cheddar cheese
salt and pepper	salt and pepper
grated nutmeg	grated nutmeg

Melt the butter in a saucepan, stir in the flour and cook for 1 minute. Remove from the heat and gradually blend in the milk. Heat, stirring, until the sauce thickens. Simmer, stirring, for 2 minutes, then remove from the heat and cool slightly. Beat in the egg yolks, cheese and salt, pepper and nutmeg to taste.

Whisk the egg whites until stiff and fold into the cheese mixture quickly. Turn into a greased 1.2 litre/2 pint soufflé dish and cook in a moderately hot oven (190°C/375°F, Gas Mark 5) for 35 to 40 minutes until well risen and golden brown. Serve immediately.
Serves 4

Stilton Soufflé

METRIC/IMPERIAL	AMERICAN
50 g/2 oz butter	¼ cup butter
50 g/2 oz plain flour	½ cup all-purpose flour
300 ml/½ pint milk	1¼ cups milk
salt and pepper	salt and pepper
3 eggs, separated	3 eggs, separated
100 g/4 oz Stilton cheese, grated	1 cup grated Stilton cheese

Prepare the soufflé mixture as for Cheese Soufflé (see above) and turn into a greased 1.2 litre/2 pint soufflé dish. Place in a moderately hot oven (190°C/375°F, Gas Mark 5) for 35 to 40 minutes until well risen and golden brown. Serve immediately.
Serves 4

Carrot Soufflé

METRIC/IMPERIAL
500 g/1 lb carrots, chopped
1 onion, chopped
450 ml/³⁄4 pint water
salt
freshly ground white pepper
25 g/1 oz margarine
1 tablespoon plain flour
150 ml/¹⁄4 pint milk
50 g/2 oz red Leicester cheese,
  finely grated
4 eggs, separated

AMERICAN
3 cups chopped carrots
1 onion, chopped
2 cups water
salt
freshly ground white pepper
2 tablespoons margarine
1 tablespoon all-purpose flour
²⁄3 cup milk
¹⁄2 cup finely grated cheese
4 eggs, separated

Place the carrots in a pan with the onion, water and salt. Bring to the boil, lower the heat, cover and simmer for 20 minutes or until the carrots are soft. Drain, then mash or purée in an electric blender. Add salt and pepper to taste.

Melt the margarine in a saucepan, add the flour and cook for 1 minute. Remove from the heat and gradually blend in the milk. Heat, stirring, until the sauce thickens.

Stir the sauce into the carrot purée with the cheese and the egg yolks. Whisk the egg whites until stiff, then fold into the carrot mixture. Pour into a greased 1.5 litre/2½ pint soufflé dish.

Cook in a moderate oven (180°C/350°F, Gas Mark 4) for 45 minutes until well risen and set. Serve immediately.
Serves 4

Note: As a starter, this soufflé will provide 6 to 8 servings.

Aubergine (Eggplant) Soufflés

METRIC/IMPERIAL
500 g/1 lb aubergines
40 g/1½ oz butter
1 tablespoon grated onion
25 g/1 oz plain flour
300 ml/½ pint milk
salt and pepper
2 eggs, separated
25 g/1 oz Parmesan cheese, grated

AMERICAN
1 lb eggplants
3 tablespoons butter
1 tablespoon grated onion
¼ cup all-purpose flour
1¼ cups milk
salt and pepper
2 eggs, separated
¼ cup grated Parmesan cheese

Bake the aubergines (eggplants) in a moderate oven (180°C/350°F, Gas Mark 4) for 40 to 45 minutes or until soft. Remove the skin and chop the aubergine (eggplant) flesh.

Melt the butter in a large pan, add the onion and cook for 1 minute. Add the aubergine (eggplant) and mix well. Stir in the flour and cook for 1 minute. Remove from the heat and gradually blend in the milk. Heat, stirring, until the sauce thickens. Add salt and pepper to taste.

Beat in the egg yolks and half the Parmesan cheese. Whisk the egg whites until stiff and fold into the mixture. Divide between 4 greased individual 7.5 cm/3 inch soufflé dishes. Sprinkle with the remaining cheese and place in a moderate oven (180°C/350°F, Gas Mark 4) for 20 to 25 minutes until risen and golden. Serve immediately.
Serves 4

Note: To serve as a starter, rather than a main course, the above quantities will serve 6. Divide the mixture between 6 ramekin dishes and bake as above for 15 to 20 minutes.

COLD SOUFFLÉS

Apricot Soufflé

METRIC/IMPERIAL	AMERICAN
225 g/8 oz dried apricots	*1 ⅓ cups dried apricots*
300 ml/½ pint boiling water	*1 ¼ cups boiling water*
3 eggs, separated	*3 eggs, separated*
100 g/4 oz caster sugar	*½ cup sugar*
5 tablespoons water	*5 tablespoons water*
15 g/½ oz gelatine	*2 envelopes gelatin*
4 tablespoons apricot brandy	*4 tablespoons apricot brandy*
2 teaspoons lemon juice	*2 teaspoons lemon juice*
300 ml/½ pint double cream,	*1 ¼ cups heavy cream, whipped*
* whipped*	

Prepare a 15 cm/6 inch soufflé dish (see page 10).

Cover the apricots with the boiling water. Leave to soak for 1 hour, then transfer the apricots and water to a saucepan. Simmer gently until the fruit is soft, then purée in an electric blender or press through a sieve (strainer).

Place the egg yolks and sugar in a bowl over a pan of hot water. Whisk until the mixture is thick and creamy, remove from the heat and whisk until cool.

Place the water in a small bowl and add the gelatine. Place over a pan of hot water and stir until the gelatine is dissolved. Fold into the egg mixture with the fruit purée, brandy and lemon juice.

Reserve one third of the cream for decoration and fold the remainder into the apricot mixture. Whisk the egg whites until stiff and fold into the soufflé mixture evenly. Turn into the soufflé dish and leave in a cool place until set.

To serve, carefully remove the collar and decorate the soufflé with piped cream rosettes.

Serves 6

APRICOT SOUFFLÉ, BLACKBERRY SOUFFLÉS *(page 54)*
(Photograph: British Sugar Bureau)

Black Cherry Soufflé

METRIC/IMPERIAL	AMERICAN
4 eggs, separated	4 eggs, separated
100 g/4 oz caster sugar	½ cup sugar
15 g/½ oz gelatine	2 envelopes gelatin
5 tablespoons water	5 tablespoons water
300 ml/½ pint double cream, lightly whipped	1¼ cups heavy cream, lightly whipped
225 g/8 oz fresh or frozen black cherries, stoned and chopped	½ lb fresh or frozen bing cherries, pitted and chopped
toasted nuts to decorate	toasted nuts to decorate

Prepare a 15 cm/6 inch soufflé dish (see page 10).

Place the egg yolks and sugar in a bowl over a pan of hot water and whisk until thick and creamy. Remove from the heat and whisk until cool.

Put the water in a small bowl and add the gelatine. Place over a pan of hot water and stir until dissolved. Cool slightly, then fold into the egg mixture, with two thirds of the cream and the fruit.

Whisk the egg whites until stiff and fold into the mixture. Turn into the soufflé dish and leave in a cool place until set.

To serve, carefully remove the collar and press the nuts around the side of the soufflé. Decorate the top with the reserved cream.
Serves 4 to 6

Blackberry Soufflés

METRIC/IMPERIAL	AMERICAN
500 g/1 lb fresh or frozen blackberries, thawed	1 lb fresh or frozen blackberries, thawed
4 eggs, separated	4 eggs, separated
100 g/4 oz caster sugar	½ cup sugar
5 tablespoons water	5 tablespoons water
15 g/½ oz gelatine	2 envelopes gelatin
300 ml/½ pint double cream, whipped	1¼ cups heavy cream, whipped

Prepare six 7.5 cm/3 inch individual soufflé dishes (see page 10).

Reserve 6 blackberries for decoration and purée the rest in an electric blender, then sieve to remove the pips. Prepare the soufflé mixture as for Black Cherry Soufflé (see above). Divide between the soufflé dishes and leave in a cool place until set. Decorate with the reserved cream and blackberries.
Serves 6

Coffee Praline Soufflé

METRIC/IMPERIAL
150 g/5 oz sugar
2 tablespoons water
50 g/2 oz unblanched whole
 almonds
3 eggs, separated
150 ml/¼ pint milk
2 tablespoons Tia Maria or brandy
1 tablespoon gelatine
5 tablespoons water
150 ml/¼ pint double cream
150 ml/¼ pint single cream
toasted flaked almonds to decorate

AMERICAN
⅔ cup sugar
2 tablespoons water
⅓ cup unblanched whole almonds
3 eggs, separated
⅔ cup milk
2 tablespoons Tia Maria or brandy
1 tablespoon gelatin
5 tablespoons water
⅔ cup heavy cream
⅔ cup light cream
toasted flaked almonds to decorate

Prepare a 15 cm/6 inch soufflé dish (see page 10).

To make the praline, place the sugar and water in a saucepan and heat until the sugar has dissolved. Bring to the boil, add the nuts and boil until the syrup is a rich golden brown. Pour onto an oiled baking sheet or marble slab. When cold, crush the praline with a rolling pin.

Place the egg yolks, milk and liqueur in a bowl over hot water. Cook, stirring, until the mixture thickens.

Put the water in a small bowl and sprinkle over the gelatine. Place over a pan of hot water and stir until dissolved. Cool slightly and stir into the egg mixture. Leave until just beginning to set.

Whip the double and single creams together until just stiff. Reserve one third for decoration and fold the remainder into the soufflé mixture. Whisk the egg whites until stiff and fold into the soufflé mixture with the crushed praline. Turn into the soufflé dish and leave in a cool place until set.

To serve, carefully remove the collar and press the almonds around the side of the soufflé. Decorate the top with piped whipped cream.

Serves 6

Orange and Lemon Soufflé

METRIC/IMPERIAL
4 eggs, separated
100 g/4 oz light soft brown sugar
finely grated rind and juice of
  2 lemons
finely grated rind and juice of
  2 oranges
15 g/½ oz gelatine
150 ml/¼ pint natural yogurt

AMERICAN
4 eggs, separated
⅔ cup light brown sugar
finely grated rind and juice of
  2 lemons
finely grated rind and juice of
  2 oranges
2 envelopes gelatin
⅔ cup unflavored yogurt

Prepare an 18 cm/7 inch soufflé dish (see page 10).

Put the egg yolks, sugar, lemon rind and juice, orange rind and half the orange juice in a bowl. Place the bowl over a pan of simmering water and whisk until thick. Remove from the heat and continue whisking until cool.

Put the remaining orange juice in a bowl and sprinkle over the gelatine. Stand over a pan of hot water and stir until the gelatine is dissolved.

Stir the gelatine and yogurt into the egg mixture, then leave in a cool place until beginning to set. Whisk the egg whites until just stiff and fold quickly into the mixture. Pour into the soufflé dish and leave in a cool place until set. Remove the collar carefully before serving.
Serves 4 to 6

Orange and Almond Soufflé
Follow the above recipe, but use the grated rind and juice of 3 oranges and 1 lemon. Replace the brown sugar with caster sugar and add a few drops of almond essence (extract) to the soufflé mixture with the yogurt.

When the soufflé is set, remove the collar and press 2 to 3 tablespoons macaroon crumbs around the sides. Decorate the top with piped whipped cream, toasted split almonds and orange slices.

Milanese Soufflés

METRIC/IMPERIAL
3 eggs, separated
75 g/3 oz caster sugar
1 tablespoon gelatine
2 tablespoons water
finely grated rind and juice of
 2 lemons
150 ml/¼ pint double cream,
 lightly whipped
To decorate:
25 g/1 oz walnuts, finely chopped
whipped cream
mimosa balls

AMERICAN
3 eggs, separated
6 tablespoons sugar
1 tablespoon gelatin
2 tablespoons water
finely grated rind and juice of
 2 lemons
⅔ cup heavy cream, lightly
 whipped
To decorate:
¼ cup finely chopped walnuts
whipped cream
mimosa balls

Prepare four 7.5 cm/3 inch individual soufflé dishes (see page 10).

Place the egg yolks and sugar in a bowl and whisk until pale and thick. Put the water in a small bowl and sprinkle over the gelatine. Stand over a pan of hot water and stir until dissolved. Cool slightly, then whisk into the egg mixture with the lemon rind and juice. Leave in a cool place until just beginning to set, stirring occasionally.

Fold the cream into the soufflé mixture. Whisk the egg whites until stiff and fold in evenly. Divide the mixture between the soufflé dishes and leave in a cool place until set.

To serve, carefully remove the collars and press the chopped walnuts around the side of the soufflés. Decorate the tops with whipped cream and mimosa balls.
Serves 4

Individual Orange Soufflés
Prepare the soufflés as above, replacing the lemons with oranges. Decorate the sides with chopped walnuts and the tops with whipped cream and orange slices.

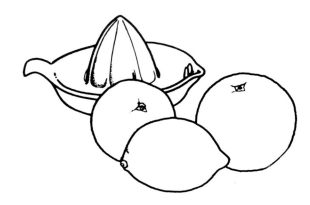

Chestnut Soufflé

METRIC/IMPERIAL
4 eggs, separated
50 g/2 oz sugar
15 g/½ oz gelatine
4 tablespoons water
227 g/8 oz can sweetened chestnut
  purée
150 ml/¼ pint double cream,
  whipped
3-4 tablespoons Amaretto di
  Saronno liqueur or brandy
To decorate:
whipped cream
whole marrons glacés

AMERICAN
4 eggs, separated
¼ cup sugar
2 envelopes gelatin
4 tablespoons water
½ lb can sweetened chestnut paste
⅔ cup heavy cream, whipped
3-4 tablespoons Amaretto di
  Saronno liqueur or brandy
To decorate:
whipped cream
whole marrons glacés

Prepare a 15 cm/6 inch soufflé dish (see page 10).

Place the egg yolks and sugar in a bowl and whisk until thick and pale in colour. Put the water in a small bowl and sprinkle over the gelatine. Place over a pan of hot water and stir until dissolved. Cool slightly, then stir into the egg mixture with the chestnut purée (paste). Fold in the cream together with the liqueur. Whisk the egg whites until stiff and carefully fold into the soufflé mixture.

Turn the mixture into the soufflé dish and leave in a cool place until set. To serve, carefully remove the collar and decorate the soufflé with whipped cream and whole marrons glacés.
Serves 6

Ginger Soufflé
Prepare the soufflé mixture as above, replacing the chestnut purée (paste) with ½ teaspoon ground ginger and 25 g/1 oz (¼ cup) chopped preserved stem ginger. Use 4 tablespoons ginger wine in place of the liqueur. Decorate the soufflé with crystallized (candied) ginger slices.

HOT DESSERTS

Each of the following quick and easy fillings is enough to fill 8 hot crêpes made from 300 ml/½ pint (1¼ cups) crêpe batter (see page 8). Quantities are sufficient to serve 4.

Apple Crêpes with Cream
Cook 500 g/1 lb peeled, cored and sliced cooking apples with ½ teaspoon ground cinnamon and 4 tablespoons rose hip syrup until soft and pulpy, then beat to a smooth purée.

Divide the mixture between the crêpes, roll up and arrange in a warmed serving dish. Sprinkle with sugar and top with 150 ml/ ¼ pint (⅔ cup) whipped double (heavy) cream. Serve immediately.

Apricot and Hazelnut (Filbert) Crêpes
Place the contents of 1 × 425 g/15 oz can apricot pie filling in a saucepan with 50 g/2 oz (½ cup) chopped hazelnuts (filberts) and 1 tablespoon demerara (raw) sugar. Heat through gently and divide the mixture between the crêpes. Fold into quarters and arrange in a warmed heatproof serving dish. Sprinkle liberally with demerara (raw) sugar and place under a hot grill (broiler) until the sugar begins to melt. Serve immediately.

Chestnut Crêpes
Heat 1 × 200 g/7 oz can sweetened chestnut purée (paste) until soft. Cool slightly, then beat in 150 ml/¼ pint (⅔ cup) whipped double (heavy) cream. Blend in 2 tablespoons sherry and spread the mixture over the crêpes. Fold into quarters, dust with icing (confectioners') sugar and serve immediately.

Crêpes aux Cerises
Soak 225 g/½ lb stoned black (pitted bing) cherries in 4 tablespoons Amaretto di Saronno liqueur or Kirsch overnight. Divide the mixture between the crêpes, roll up and arrange in an ovenproof serving dish. Sprinkle liberally with flaked almonds and sifted icing (confectioners') sugar. Place in a hot oven (200°C/400°F, Gas Mark 6) for 10 minutes. Serve immediately with cream.

APPLE CRÊPES WITH CREAM
(Photograph: Delrosa)

Grapefruit and Brandy Crêpes
Grate the rind from 2 grapefruits, then divide into segments, removing all pith. Place the grapefruit rind in a saucepan with 50 g/2 oz (¼ cup) sugar and 2 tablespoons water. Bring to the boil and boil for 2 minutes. Add 2 to 3 tablespoons brandy and the grapefruit segments. Divide the mixture between the crêpes, roll up and arrange in a warmed serving dish. Dust with icing (confectioners') sugar and serve immediately.

Pineapple and Vanilla Crêpes
Drain 1 × 425 g/15 oz can pineapple chunks and add the fruit to 300 ml/½ pint (1¼ cups) cold custard. Stir in 25 g/1 oz (¼ cup) sifted icing (confectioners') sugar and 1 teaspoon vanilla essence (extract). Divide the mixture between the crêpes and roll up. Arrange in a warmed serving dish. Dust with icing (confectioners') sugar and serve immediately.

Plum Cream Crêpes
Whip 300 ml/½ pint (1¼ cups) double (heavy) cream until stiff and add 2 teaspoons Kirsch. Fold 350 g/¾ lb stoned (pitted) and chopped dessert plums into the cream. Divide the mixture between the crêpes, roll up and arrange in a warmed serving dish. Dust with icing (confectioners') sugar and serve immediately.

Rum and Banana Crêpes
Mash 4 bananas with 2 teaspoons lemon juice and 2 tablespoons sugar. Blend 2 teaspoons cornflour (cornstarch) with 150 ml/ ¼ pint (⅔ cup) rum in a saucepan. Heat, stirring, until the mixture thickens. Stir in the bananas and cook for 1 minute. Divide the mixture between the crêpes, roll up, arrange in a warmed serving dish and dust with sugar. Serve hot.

Flambéed Raspberry Crêpes

METRIC/IMPERIAL
8 crêpes (see page 8)
500 g/1 lb fresh or frozen
  raspberries, thawed
75 g/3 oz butter
50 g/2 oz caster sugar
4 tablespoons Galliano or Kirsch
2 tablespoons lemon juice

AMERICAN
8 crêpes (see page 8)
1 lb fresh or frozen raspberries,
  thawed
⅓ cup butter
¼ cup sugar
4 tablespoons Galliano or Kirsch
2 tablespoons lemon juice

Make up the crêpes and keep warm. Place the raspberries in a large flameproof gratin dish and heat through gently.

Beat the butter and sugar together until light and fluffy. Blend in half of the liqueur and the lemon juice. Divide between the crêpes, spoon the raspberries on top and fold each crêpe into quarters.

Place the crêpes in the gratin dish and heat gently for 5 to 10 minutes; the filling will melt to make a sauce.

Before serving, pour the rest of the liqueur into a warmed ladle, ignite and pour over the crêpes. Serve immediately.
Serves 4

Apple and Almond Crêpe Layer

METRIC/IMPERIAL
8 crêpes (see page 8)
25 g/1 oz butter
750 g/1 ½ lb cooking apples,
  peeled, cored and sliced
1 tablespoon water
50 g/2 oz sugar
50 g/2 oz flaked almonds, toasted
6 tablespoons plum jam

AMERICAN
8 crêpes (see page 8)
2 tablespoons butter
1 ½ lb baking apples, peeled, cored
  and sliced
1 tablespoon water
¼ cup sugar
½ cup flaked and toasted almonds
6 tablespoons plum jam

Make up the crêpes and keep warm.

Melt the butter in a saucepan and add the apples, water and sugar. Cook gently until the apples are just tender. Stir in half the almonds.

Place one crêpe on a heatproof serving plate and spread with a little jam and some of the apple mixture. Place a crêpe on top, and continue with these layers, finishing with a crêpe. Cover with foil and place in a moderate oven (180°C/350°F, Gas Mark 4) for 5 to 10 minutes to heat through. Decorate with the remaining almonds and serve with cream.
Serves 4

Wholewheat Honey Crêpes

METRIC/IMPERIAL	AMERICAN
100 g/4 oz wholemeal self-raising flour	1 cup wholewheat self-rising flour
1 egg, beaten	1 egg, beaten
300 ml/½ pint milk	1¼ cups milk
4 tablespoons clear honey	¼ cup clear honey
50 g/2 oz seedless raisins	⅓ cup seedless raisins
pinch of grated nutmeg	pinch of grated nutmeg

Put the flour in a bowl and make a well in the centre. Pour in the egg and milk and beat to a smooth batter. Mix together the honey, raisins and nutmeg.

Using a lightly oiled frying pan (skillet) and the batter, cook 8 crêpes (see page 8); keep warm. Spread each crêpe with a spoonful of the honey mixture, then fold to form wedge-shaped parcels. Serve immediately.

Serves 4

Crunchy Apricot Fritters

METRIC/IMPERIAL	AMERICAN
8 crêpes (see page 8)	8 crêpes (see page 8)
8 tablespoons apricot jam	8 tablespoons apricot jam
50 g/2 oz breadcrumbs	½ cup bread crumbs
50 g/2 oz cornflakes, crushed	2 cups crushed cornflakes
1 egg, beaten	1 egg, beaten
oil for shallow frying	oil for shallow frying
25 g/1 oz caster sugar	2 tablespoons sugar
1 teaspoon ground cinnamon	1 teaspoon ground cinnamon

Make up the crêpes, spread each one with jam and roll up firmly. Trim the ends of the crêpes and cut each one in half.

Mix together the breadcrumbs and cornflakes. Coat each piece of crêpe in beaten egg, then in the crumb mixture. Heat the oil in a frying pan (skillet) and fry the coated crêpes until golden brown. Remove from the pan, drain well and arrange on a warmed serving plate. Sprinkle the sugar and cinnamon over the fritters. Serve hot, with cream.

Serves 4

Orange and Cream Cheese Crêpes

METRIC/IMPERIAL
8 crêpes (see page 8)
Filling:
175 g/6 oz cream cheese
2 tablespoons single cream
2 tablespoons clear honey
50 g/2 oz sultanas
grated rind of 1 orange
Sauce:
juice of 2 oranges
150 ml/¼ pint water
  (approximately)
grated rind of 1 orange
1 tablespoon arrowroot
25 g/1 oz soft brown sugar
1 tablespoon clear honey
To decorate:
orange slices

AMERICAN
8 crêpes (see page 8)
Filling:
¾ cup cream cheese
2 tablespoons light cream
2 tablespoons clear honey
⅓ cup seedless white raisins
grated rind of 1 orange
Sauce:
juice of 2 oranges
⅔ cup water (approximately)
grated rind of 1 orange
1 tablespoon arrowroot flour
3 tablespoons light brown sugar
1 tablespoon clear honey
To decorate:
orange slices

Make up the crêpes and keep warm.

Place all the filling ingredients in a bowl and beat until well blended.

To make the sauce, place the orange juice in a measuring jug and make up to 300 ml/½ pint (1¼ cups) with the water. Place the orange rind and arrowroot in a small pan and gradually blend in the orange juice. Stir in the sugar and honey. Heat, stirring, until the sauce thickens. Simmer, stirring, for 1 minute.

Divide the filling between the crêpes and roll up. Pile onto a warmed serving dish and pour a little sauce over the crêpes. Decorate with orange slices and serve the remaining sauce separately.
Serves 4

Crêpes Suzette

METRIC/IMPERIAL
8 crêpes made from enriched batter
  (see page 8)
50 g/2 oz sugar cubes
2 oranges
1 tablespoon water
50 g/2 oz butter
2-3 tablespoons Grand Marnier or
  Cointreau
1 tablespoon brandy
orange twists to decorate

AMERICAN
8 crêpes made from enriched batter
  (see page 8)
2 oz lump sugar
2 oranges
1 tablespoon water
¼ cup butter
2-3 tablespoons Grand Marnier or
  Cointreau
1 tablespoon brandy
orange twists to decorate

Make up the crêpes and set aside.

Rub the sugar cubes (lumps) over the oranges until they have absorbed the zest and are yellow, then place the sugar in a pan with the water. Heat until dissolved, then boil until golden brown.

Squeeze the juice from the oranges and add to the pan. Bring to the boil, lower the heat and simmer for 1 minute then add the butter and liqueur.

Heat the crêpes in the sauce individually, fold into quarters and keep warm. Return them all to the pan and pour over the brandy. Set alight and serve immediately, decorated with orange twists.
Serves 4

Apple Omelets

METRIC/IMPERIAL
Filling:
50 g/2 oz butter
2 tablespoons apricot jam
2 cooking apples, peeled, cored and
  sliced
25 g/1 oz caster sugar
Omelets:
4 eggs, separated
25 g/1 oz caster sugar
2 teaspoons cornflour
½ teaspoon vanilla essence
25 g/1 oz unsalted butter
To finish:
caster sugar for sprinkling

AMERICAN
Filling:
¼ cup butter
2 tablespoons apricot jam
2 baking apples, peeled, cored and
  sliced
2 tablespoons sugar
Omelets:
4 eggs, separated
2 tablespoons sugar
2 teaspoons cornstarch
½ teaspoon vanilla extract
2 tablespoons sweet butter
To finish:
sugar for sprinkling

Place the butter and apricot jam in a saucepan and heat gently until the butter is melted. Add the apples, cover and cook gently until they are just soft, then stir in the sugar.

To make the omelets, whisk together the egg yolks, sugar, cornflour (cornstarch) and vanilla essence (extract) until thick and creamy. Whisk the egg whites until stiff and fold into the mixture.

Melt half of the butter in a 23 cm/9 inch frying pan (skillet). When it is just sizzling, pour in half the egg mixture. Cook slowly, without stirring, until the omelet is just golden underneath and the sides are beginning to set. Place the pan under a hot grill (broiler) until the top is golden.

Make a slit across the centre of the omelet, spoon half of the apple mixture onto one side of the omelet and fold over. Sprinkle with sugar. Cut in half and slide onto a warmed serving plate. Keep warm while making another omelet with the remaining ingredients. Serve immediately, with cream.
Serves 4

APPLE OMELETS
(Photograph: British Sugar Bureau)

Lemon Soufflé Galliano

METRIC/IMPERIAL
50 g/2 oz sugar
3 tablespoons plain flour
175 ml/6 fl oz milk
4 egg yolks, lightly beaten
50 g/2 oz unsalted butter
4 tablespoons Galliano or
  Cointreau
1 teaspoon grated lemon rind
1 tablespoon lemon juice
5 egg whites
pinch of salt

AMERICAN
¼ cup sugar
3 tablespoons all-purpose flour
¾ cup milk
4 egg yolks, lightly beaten
¼ cup sweet butter
4 tablespoons Galliano or
  Cointreau
1 teaspoon grated lemon rind
1 tablespoon lemon juice
5 egg whites
pinch of salt

Prepare an 18 cm/7 inch soufflé dish as for a chilled soufflé (see page 10). Sprinkle the oiled dish and collar with a little of the sugar.

Place the remaining sugar and flour in a saucepan and blend with a little of the milk. Stir in the remaining milk and heat, stirring, until the sauce thickens. Continue to cook for 1 minute, then cool slightly and gradually beat in the egg yolks and the butter. Heat, stirring, until the mixture becomes thick and smooth. Transfer to a large bowl and blend in the liqueur, lemon rind and juice.

Whisk the egg whites with the salt until stiff and fold into the lemon mixture, using a metal spoon. Turn into the soufflé dish and place in a moderately hot oven (190°C/375°F, Gas Mark 5) for 45 minutes or until the soufflé is well risen and firm. Serve immediately.
Serves 6

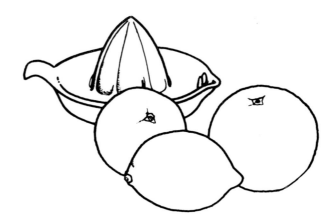

Orange Soufflé with Sauce

METRIC/IMPERIAL
Soufflé:
50 g/2 oz butter
40 g/1½ oz plain flour
300 ml/½ pint milk
grated rind of 2 oranges
4 eggs, separated
40 g/1½ oz sugar
Sauce:
grated rind and juice of 1 orange
300 ml/½ pint water
2 teaspoons arrowroot
25 g/1 oz sugar
To decorate:
orange segments

AMERICAN
Soufflé
¼ cup butter
6 tablespoons all-purpose flour
1¼ cups milk
grated rind of 2 oranges
4 eggs, separated
3 tablespoons sugar
Sauce:
grated rind and juice of 1 orange
1¼ cups water
2 teaspoons arrowroot flour
2 tablespoons sugar
To decorate:
orange segments

Melt the butter in a saucepan, stir in the flour and cook for 1 minute. Remove from the heat and blend in the milk. Return to the heat and stir until the sauce thickens. Continue to cook for 1 to 2 minutes. Cool slightly and beat in the orange rind, egg yolks and sugar.

Whisk the egg whites until stiff and fold into the orange mixture. Turn into a greased 18 cm/7 inch soufflé dish. Place in a moderately hot oven (200°C/400°F, Gas Mark 6) for 35 to 40 minutes or until well risen and firm.

To make the sauce, place all the ingredients in a saucepan. Heat, whisking, until the sauce thickens. Add a little extra water if it is too thick and continue to cook for 1 minute. Decorate the soufflé with orange segments and hand the sauce separately. Serve immediately.
Serves 4 to 6

Harvest Fruit Soufflé Omelets

METRIC/IMPERIAL
8 eggs, separated
50 g/2 oz caster sugar
few drops of vanilla essence
50 g/2 oz butter
1 × 400 g/15 oz can black cherries,
  drained and stoned
To finish:
sifted icing sugar

AMERICAN
8 eggs, separated
¼ cup sugar
few drops of vanilla extract
¼ cup butter
1 × 15 oz can bing cherries,
  drained and pitted
To finish:
sifted confectioners' sugar

Beat together the egg yolks, sugar and vanilla essence (extract) until thick and creamy. Whisk the egg whites until stiff and fold into the egg mixture.

Melt a quarter of the butter in an omelet pan. When it is sizzling add a quarter of the egg mixture. Cook over a medium heat, without stirring, for 1 to 2 minutes until the omelet is set and golden underneath.

Place the pan under a hot grill (broiler) for 1 to 2 minutes until the top of the omelet is risen and golden. Place 2 tablespoons black cherries on the omelet and fold over. Slide onto a warmed serving plate and keep warm while making 3 more omelets with the remaining ingredients. Dust with icing (confectioners') sugar and serve immediately.
Serves 4

Jam Soufflé Omelets

METRIC/IMPERIAL
8 eggs, separated
50 g/2 oz caster sugar
50 g/2 oz butter
8 tablespoons raspberry jam,
  warmed
25 g/1 oz icing sugar, sifted

AMERICAN
8 eggs, separated
¼ cup sugar
¼ cup butter
8 tablespoons raspberry jam,
  warmed
¼ cup sifted confectioners' sugar

Prepare and cook as for Harvest Fruit Soufflé Omelets (see above), using an ovenproof pan. Instead of finishing under the grill (broiler), place the pan in a moderate oven (180°C/350°F, Gas Mark 4) for 8 to 10 minutes until the omelet is risen and firm to touch. Repeat with the remaining omelets.

Spread with the jam and fold in half. Slide the omelets onto warmed serving plates. Dust with icing (confectioners') sugar and serve immediately.
Serves 4

TANGY CHICKEN CRÊPES *(page 27)*,
HARVEST FRUIT SOUFFLÉ OMELETS
(Photograph: Pointerware (UK) Limited)

Hot Chocolate Soufflé

METRIC/IMPERIAL	AMERICAN
25 g/1 oz butter	2 tablespoons butter
2 tablespoons plain flour	2 tablespoons all-purpose flour
2 tablespoons cornflour	2 tablespoons cornstarch
300 ml/½ pint milk	1¼ cups milk
50 g/2 oz caster sugar	¼ cup sugar
3 egg yolks	3 egg yolks
100 g/4 oz plain chocolate	⅔ cup semi-sweet chocolate pieces
4 egg whites	4 egg whites

Melt the butter in a saucepan, add the flour and cornflour (cornstarch) and cook for 1 minute. Remove from the heat and gradually blend in the milk. Heat, stirring, until the sauce thickens, then cool slightly and beat in the sugar and egg yolks.

Break the chocolate, add to the sauce and stir until melted.

Whisk the egg whites until stiff and fold into the chocolate mixture. Turn the mixture into a greased 18 cm/7 inch soufflé dish. Place in a moderately hot oven (190°C/375°F, Gas Mark 5) for 35 minutes until well risen and firm. Serve immediately, with cream.
Serves 4 to 6

Rhubarb and Ginger Soufflé

METRIC/IMPERIAL	AMERICAN
500 g/1 lb rhubarb, trimmed	1 lb rhubarb, trimmed
50 g/2 oz sugar	¼ cup sugar
50 g/2 oz butter	¼ cup butter
50 g/2 oz breadcrumbs	¼ cup bread crumbs
200 ml/⅓ pint milk	1 cup milk
4 eggs, separated	4 eggs, separated
½ teaspoon ground ginger	½ teaspoon ground ginger

Chop the rhubarb, place in a saucepan and add 2 tablespoons of the sugar and a few drops of water. Cook gently until the fruit is soft. Strain off most of the liquid.

Place the butter, breadcrumbs and milk in a saucepan. Heat, whisking, for 2 to 3 minutes until smooth. Cool slightly, then beat in the egg yolks, remaining sugar, ginger and rhubarb. Whisk the egg whites until stiff and fold into the mixture. Turn into a greased 15 cm/6 inch soufflé dish. Cook in a moderately hot oven (200°C/400°F, Gas Mark 6) for 35 to 40 minutes until well risen. Serve immediately, with cream.
Serves 4

Almond Soufflé

METRIC/IMPERIAL	AMERICAN
50 g/2 oz butter	*¼ cup butter*
50 g/2 oz plain flour	*½ cup all-purpose flour*
3 tablespoons milk	*3 tablespoons milk*
5 eggs, separated	*5 eggs, separated*
1 tablespoon sugar	*1 tablespoon sugar*
5 tablespoons Amaretto di Saronno	*5 tablespoons Amaretto di Saronno*
liqueur	*liqueur*
4 macaroons	*4 macaroons*
few flaked almonds to decorate	*few flaked almonds to decorate*

Prepare a 15 cm/6 inch soufflé dish as for a chilled soufflé (see page 10).

Melt the butter in a saucepan and add the flour. Cook for 1 minute, then blend in the milk and cook, stirring, for a further 1 minute. Allow to cool slightly. Beat the egg yolks thoroughly, then add to the white sauce with the sugar and 3 tablespoons of the liqueur and beat well. Soak the macaroons in the remaining liqueur and set aside.

Whisk the egg whites until stiff, then fold into the sauce evenly. Arrange the soaked macaroons in the soufflé dish and pour the mixture over the top. Sprinkle with the almonds and place in a moderately hot oven (190°C/375°F, Gas Mark 5) for 30 minutes until well risen. Remove the collar and serve immediately.

Serves 4 to 6

INDEX

The publishers wish to acknowledge the following photographers: Melvin Grey: 21;
Paul Kemp: 49; Roger Phillips: 57, 65; Paul Williams: 9, 17, 33, 37, 73 and cover.